Adam Ferguson *by Raeburn*

EDINBURGH

IN THE AGE OF

REASON

a commemoration

by

DOUGLAS YOUNG

A. J. YOUNGSON

GEORGE E. DAVIE

DUNCAN FORBES

THE HON. LORD CAMERON

ALLAN FRAZER

1967

at the University Press

EDINBURGH

Preface

The essays in this book were planned as a series of talks for broadcasting as a contribution to the celebration of the bicentenary of the New Town of Edinburgh and as an acknowledgment of the second International Congress on the Enlightenment held at St Andrews University this month. It is also appropriate that comment should be made on the occasion of the bicentenary of the publication of Adam Ferguson's *Essay on the History of Civil Society*, a book whose central position in the 'Enlightenment' dialogue made its neglect, until its reissue by the University Press last year, difficult to understand. The talks were broadcast in *Scottish Life and Letters* on the Scottish Home Service of the BBC between January and June 1967.

George Bruce, Producer, Scottish Life & Letters
August 1967

Contents

Introduction

Douglas Young

The Scottish Enlightenment is an important part of that international movement, of the seventeenth and eighteenth centuries, which is also called the Age of Reason, because many intellectuals at that period shared a general optimism about the powers of human reasoning to discover the workings of the Universe, and to perfect human nature and human society in a world created by a reasonable and good 'Architect of the Universe'.

The roots of the Enlightenment run right back to some of the Greek city-states of the sixth century BC; the movement had been fostered by the invention of printing in the fifteenth century, and the wide diffusion of Greek and Latin works of science, philosophy, medicine, and literature. These promoted intellectual liberation, and a freer criticism of beliefs and practices surviving from the Middle Ages, leading both to religious wars for a century and a half, and to technological improvements, which made possible a more agreeable life in this world for increasing numbers of people, especially, of course, the upper classes of society.

It was in Edinburgh, in the last quarter of the eighteenth

century, that the Scottish Enlightenment kindled into flame. Benjamin Constant, the author of *Adolphe*, whose powers of self-analysis and realism may well have been sharpened when he was a student at the University of Edinburgh in its greatest years, describes the intellectual milieu:

Arrived at this city on the 8th of July 1782 . . . I applied myself to my studies with great fervour; and now began the most agreeable year of my life. Work was fashionable amongst the young people of Edinburgh. They had formed several literary and philosophical clubs. I belonged to some of these, and won distinction as a writer and orator, although in a foreign language. I established close relations with men who, for the most part, became well-known in recent years . . . Amongst all these young people, the one who seemed most promising was the son of a tobacconist, by name John Wilde. He had an almost absolute authority over all friends, although most of these were much his superiors in birth and fortune.

Constant shrewdly notices that the Scottish nation of the eighteenth century was simultaneously a more aristocratic and a more democratic community than could be found at that time in either France or England. An Englishman called Amyat, who was official Chemist to George III, made a similar comment on the intellectual democracy of Edinburgh, where '. . . the access of men of parts is not only easy, but their conversation and the communication of their knowledge are at once imparted to intelligent strangers with the utmost liberality. The philosophers of Scotland have no *nostrums*. They tell what they know, and deliver their sentiments without disguise or reserve.'

Something of this no doubt derived from the peculiar social structure which achieved its physical expression in the tall tenements of the Old Town. Scotland had a relatively large aristocratic class, most of the 150 or so peerage families

8

ramifying into large clans, with hundreds or thousands of persons in the middle and lower income groups able to claim cousinship with the noble lords at the top. The bulk of the nation was a hardy peasantry, distinguished by a zeal for education and self-improvement fostered by the Calvinist Presbyterian Kirk.

By the middle of the eighteenth century Edinburgh had become the winter-quarters of the wealthier Scots land-owners, who mingled there with their cousins, the lawyers and medical men and ministers of religion, many of whom had taken courses in Dutch universities. In the Old Town, along the ridge from Edinburgh Castle to the Palace of Holyroodhouse, they lived cheek by jowl in the tall blocks of houses, running up to sixteen storeys, with the judges and baronets and dowager countesses on the middle floors, and the lower ranks below or above. In this setting, a unique cross-fertilization constantly took place; *ideas* – as well as *manners* – were pooled in Edinburgh, and from there spread to every parish in the country.

When, in the latter half of the eighteenth century, the over-crowding of the Old Town gave impetus to the great planning experiment of the New Town of Edinburgh, it might be thought that the increasing segregation of the aristocracy and professional classes in the latter would gradually have broken down the old synthesis, and some-thing of this no doubt occurred in time. But the intention of the New Town was in part aimed precisely at maintain-ing the metropolitan character of the city, by offering the Scottish aristocracy civic conditions that would weaken for them the growing attractions of London.

Where *manners* were concerned, numerous writers agree that Edinburgh was a friendly and cultured town, with something of a French atmosphere – a New Orleans of the North, perhaps! The Scots, noted a London society hostess, Mrs Elizabeth Montagu, 'live in ye French way, *des petits soupers fins*, and they have ye easy address of the French'. Captain Topham, an Englishman, found that 'the air of mirth and vivacity, that quick penetrating look, that spirit of gaiety which distinguish the French, is equally visible in the Scotch'.

The ferment of *ideas* focused on the University of Edinburgh. Its famous Medical School, founded by men trained in Holland, gave basic instruction in the experimental sciences. The Faculty of Arts offered a general education in Latin and Greek classical literature, logic and moral philosophy, including aesthetics and sociology and economics and psychology, as they were then understood, with a markedly historical bias. Edinburgh also had the first Chair in the world in English literature. That very great American, Thomas Jefferson, writing from Paris in 1789, expressed the view, that, where science was concerned – and by science he included all branches of speculative and experimental philosophy – 'no place in the World can pretend to a competition with Edinburgh'.

Perhaps what characterized the Scots genius of the Age of Reason was its versatility and practicality. Take, for instance, that forerunner of the Enlightenment, James Dalrymple, first Viscount of Stair, who published in 1681 his great volume, *Institutions of the Law of Scotland*, 'an original amalgam of Roman law, feudal law, and (Scottish) customary law, systematized by resort to the law of nature and the Bible, and illuminated by many flashes of ideal metaphysics'. Stair has the mental grasp of Aristotle, and a much better prose style. This eminent jurist, purely as a sideline, published, in Latin, in Holland, a treatise on experimental physiology. William Cullen, Professor of Chemistry at Edinburgh, was the first man to produce a reasoned catalogue of substances used in medical treatments; but he also pioneered the chemistry of soils and manures, a branch of technology thoroughly necessary to lairds hoping to make the best of their lands. Cullen's successor as Professor of Chemistry was Joseph Black, son of a Scots wine merchant in France. Black's name is still famous in regard to latent heat and specific heat; but he was personally involved in the early Industrial Revolution, financing James Watt's experiments with steam engines. Andrew Duncan the Elder, Professor of the Institutes of Medicine, pioneered the humane treatment of lunatics in a public asylum, presided over the Caledonian Horticultural Society, which bred a famous race of Scotch gardeners; popularized sea bathing at Leith; and even, when over eighty years old, used to climb Arthur's Seat on the first of May, and celebrate the feat by what he called a poem. Another Scots doctor, James Lind, having been the first to see the value of lemon juice as a specific against scurvy, the disease from which all eighteenth century sailors suffered, proved his case by conducting a famous clinical trial in HMS *Salisbury*, the first well-controlled therapeutic test in the entire history of medicine.

While we are on the subject of navies, it is curious to recall that the Russian Navy was started by a Scotsman called Gordon, and the American Navy by another Scot, named John Paul Jones.

Enough has perhaps been said to show that the Scots thinkers of the Enlightenment not merely refused to recognize any class distinction between the pure and applied sciences, but were prepared to treat the practical applicability of their speculations as a yardstick of their merits. It is therefore natural, in the context of such a society, that it was an Edinburgh *printer*, William Smellie, who conceived the *Encyclopaedia Britannica*. As a Scottish publisher has remarked, printers, like publishers, are sciolists – they acquire a smattering of knowledge of a vast number of topics, with little profundity in any. Smellie, the printer to the Scots Enlightenment, was therefore able to envisage the kind of synthesis which an Encyclopaedia offers, and – with his Scots practicality – keen to put this kind of printerly knowledge to good use. He therefore became the guiding force of 'a society of gentlemen in Scotland', and, in 1768, produced a 'new plan, in which the different sciences and arts are digested into distinct treatises or systems'.

The same mental atmosphere pervaded the *Edinburgh Review*, founded in 1802, and edited by Francis Jeffrey, backed by the great publisher, Constable. The name of Jeffrey – linked, as it is, with those of Sydney Smith, Brougham and Horner – brings us back full circle to the lawyers. This society of the Scottish Enlightenment was one in which a famous judge, Henry Home, Lord Kames, could encompass – outwith his professional career – interests as varied as major agricultural improvements on his estate at Blairdrummond, in Perthshire, and a whole series of philosophical works, including a two-volume *Principles of Criticism*, which has just lately been reprinted in America! At the latter end of the period, another practising lawyer, Walter Scott, could add a new dimension to world literature, make a collection of ballads and songs that would be the life's work of any professional collector today, enrich the texture of historiography, and play an active, though not altogether happy, part in political life. And so with Jeffrey. Jeffrey's career was that of a practising advocate, a Whig politician, a judge, and finally a reforming Lord Advocate. The influence exercised by the *Edinburgh Review* was world-wide. Emerson recorded: 'Like most young men at that time, I was much indebted to the men of Edinburgh and of the *Edinburgh Review*.' Madame de Staël remarked in 1815: 'If some being from another climate were to come to this, and desire to know in what work the highest pitch of human intellect might be found, he ought to be shown the *Edinburgh Review*.' Yet, Jeffrey ran the *Edinburgh* as a spare-time occupation.

No doubt the legal profession had greater leisure than

their brothers in commerce, and thus greater opportunity for letters; but their range of involvement in the affairs of society, in the *polity*, was typical of the educated classes in general. The ministers, lawyers, teachers, doctors, the lairds and the merchants, considered themselves responsible for – and indeed assumed responsibility for – the life and health of the nation. They did not leave things to others, but attempted to found the whole economy on first principles that derived both from speculative thinking and from practical experience.

That very shrewd English critic, Walter Bagehot, observes: 'There appears in the genius of the Scottish people – fostered no doubt by the abstract metaphysical speculations of their universities – a power of reducing human actions to formulas or principles.' The *rationalist and humanist principles* flourished in eighteenth century Scotland, because it was an *organic* society, not a compartmentalized organization society; there was no barrier to the free flow of ideas, least of all a barrier between 'two cultures', one scientific and the other literary. The honest application of human intelligence was the accepted test for the validity of any project, be it philosophic, literary, or practical. It is hardly a surprise, then, to discover that the Scottish Enlightenment was, to a considerable degree, a criticism and revision of the movement as it had emerged, earlier, in Europe. In particular, the Scots were the first to see the dangers to a close-knit society that were emerging in the context of industrialization, with division of labour, and increasing specialization. The concept of *alienation*, as it takes shape in the works of Adam Smith and of Adam Ferguson particularly (but also, at least by implication, in Scott) is perhaps one of the most important contributions of the Scottish intellect to European consciousness.

The City of Reason
and Nature

A. J. Youngson

For hundreds of years men have been building ideal cities –
on paper. An ideal city was planned by Vitruvius in
Augustan Rome; around the middle of the fifteenth century
the first fully planned ideal city of the Renaissance was
described and illustrated by Filarete, and we know that
Leonardo da Vinci also interested himself in such a project.

From time to time circumstances have made it possible to
undertake the enormously ambitious, costly and uncertain
task of trying to build an ideal city in reality. In the Middle
Ages, for example, there were created such cities as
Villeneuve-sur-Lot, or Aigues Mortes. But to a different age
these cities appear charming or merely curious rather than
ideal; or else they lose their orderly pattern as a result of
reconstruction or haphazard expansion, and the dream becomes again only a dream.

A fresh opportunity occurred in Scotland just after the
middle of the eighteenth century. The circumstances of
Scotland at that time were highly unusual. The tempting
adventure of restoring the Stuarts, of engineering a political
revolution on the grand scale had come to a sudden and final

end at Culloden in 1746. Thus the political situation was at last quite altered. And when Scotsmen awoke to find that the future of all of them, for as long as anyone could foresee, was in a united Britain and under the house of Hanover, they realized that they were living in a new intellectual age as well.

It was the age of the philosophers, not only French philosophers like Diderot and Voltaire but also Scots philosophers like Hume and Ferguson; the age of the Enlightenment; and those who inhabited it were 'citizens of the world, looking out upon a universe seemingly brand new because so freshly flooded with light',[1] a universe in which everything seemed much simpler than had ever before been supposed, in which everything could be fashioned anew by the light of reason. So Scotsmen set out, quite deliberately as befits rational men, to reconstruct their country. And the corporation of Edinburgh, and all the enlightened citizens of Edinburgh, and many other men and women from all over Scotland began by rebuilding, or at least by building an extension of, their ancient capital.

The proposals to do this were presented in some detail in a pamphlet published in 1752, the work, evidently, of Sir Gilbert Elliot, a lawyer and one of the *literati* of the day, and George Drummond, six times Lord Provost of Edinburgh. Their aim was to build a city which, in their own words, 'should naturally become the centre of trade and commerce, of learning and the arts, of politeness, and of refinement of every kind'. They lamented the absence of 'beauty and conveniency' in the streets of the old town, of commodious private houses, of large parks and extensive walks. But they were sure that all this could be put right.

'I happened one day', wrote one of Drummond's contemporaries, 'to be standing at a window [in the Old Town] looking out to the opposite side of the North Loch, then called Barefoot's Parks, in which there was

16

not a single house to be seen. "Look at these fields",
said Provost Drummond; "you, Mr Somerville, are a
young man, and may probably live, though I will not,
to see all these fields covered with houses, forming a
splendid and magnificent city. . . . I have never lost sight
of this object since the year 1725, when I was first
elected Provost".'[2]

By the time Somerville died, a few years after 1800, the
New Town of Edinburgh was half built and half famous.
Much effort had made it possible. But its existence rested
primarily upon an act of the imagination.

The projectors of the New Town were fortunate in their
timing. The economy grew in the second half of the
eighteenth century as never before, population increased,
numerous families became comfortably off or even wealthy.
The classical style of architecture was well established, and
many Scotsmen understood it and several had contributed
to its development – architects such as William Adam,
James Gibbs and Sir James Bruce. Above all, men were
ambitious; not only for themselves, but for their country;
not only to make money, but to achieve great objects. And
therefore in extending their ancient capital they set out to
rival the best, to do as well as London, Turin, Berlin, anywhere. We know this, because they said so. To some extent
in what they did they were following the fashion; their ideas
were not original. To some extent they were trying to
escape from the past. But they knew that life was good and
that a golden age was not far off. So they stepped forward
to build a setting for life, orderly spacious and dignified.
There were to be no shops in the Town; no markets, no
businesses. Most remarkable of all, each family was to have
a house of its own, instead of only a part of one, sharing
with others, as had been the custom, a common front-door
and a common stair. All that was to go. It was to be a city of
repose, of contemplation; of learning and the arts, as they

put it in their pamphlet; largely dissociated from the Old Town by physical separation and, to some extent, by intention.

They began by building the North Bridge. This itself was a considerable undertaking, for by the standards of the day it was a large bridge; only one much larger was built in Scotland in the eighteenth century. Then, before the North Bridge was well begun, they held the competition which produced Craig's plan. That plan was formally adopted by the magistrates in the summer of 1767, and the pattern of the New Town was set. Craig's plan was for a town consisting of three principal streets, the middle one joining a square at one end of the town to a corresponding square at the other; all rectilinear in pattern with uninterrupted views of the country to north and south.

Considering the resources of Scotland at the time and the size and character of the Old Town, this was a revolutionary and enormously ambitious proposal. For half a century it was sufficient. But, as wealth and population grew far faster than anyone had foreseen, Craig's plan turned out to be only the first instalment of the New Town. It was followed by Playfair's plan, partly abortive, for a new town between Edinburgh and Leith, to be built in the neihg-bourhood of the Calton Hill; by Reid and Sibbald's new town, laid out on the slope going down from Queen Street towards the Water of Leith; this was followed later on by Raeburn's little community development, out in the country beside and mostly beyond Stockbridge; and finally by the Earl of Moray's magnificent development of the lands of Drumsheugh.

But still, as the town grew, it retained its character, even developed it. To begin with, the private houses were not particularly elegant, and it was the monotony as much as the regularity of the street frontages which impressed ob-servers. But as time passed the houses became finer and more handsome; witness the splendid elevations of Char-

18

lotte Square and Moray Place. Magnificent public buildings also arose – Register House, one of Robert Adam's great designs, the new University building, and the National Gallery at the foot of the Mound, by Playfair.

Edinburgh began to look not only orderly, spacious and dignified, but beautiful, and even, as Lord Provost Drummond had dreamed, magnificent. And this evolution of Edinburgh as a handsome scenic town was a conscious thing. The leading citizens of Edinburgh – 'gentlemen of taste' – developed, although perhaps they had it from the first, a care for the look of things, for views and scenery. Edinburgh is not a beautiful town by accident. Undoubtedly it has a beautiful setting. It is also true that any town which is built on hills or along a river has a good chance of becoming a beautiful town. But the site guarantees nothing. There are hideous towns built on hills and along rivers. (What, for that matter, has Edinburgh made of the Water of Leith? It has wasted an excellent opportunity.) But, although that is an example of waste in Edinburgh, the men who built the New Town were on the whole most careful about preserving views and improving appearances.

The prolonged struggle to prevent building on the south side of Princes Street, a struggle which began almost as soon as Craig's plan had been accepted and which lasted for half a century, is the best known example of this. But there was also the lengthy dispute about what should be done concerning the earthen mound, as they called it. There was Starke's *Observations*, published in 1814, about the planning principles which should govern development of the Calton Hill area, putting great emphasis on the importance of retaining trees and views, having accessible walks and parks. There was a row over the North Bridge buildings at the beginning of the nineteenth century, when it was discovered that some 'glorious prospects', as Cockburn called them, looking westward from the Calton Hill would be

19

spoiled. There was trouble over the railway line going through the Princess Street gardens in the 1830s. Time and time again this question of how the town would look and what it would look out on, was raised; and every time, or at least every important time, those who were in favour of scenic advantage won. Sacrifices, sometimes considerable sacrifices, were made for the sake of how things would look. And it is because of this concern for appearances, for 'glorious prospects', that Edinburgh is a beautiful town and possesses a marvellous combination of handsome buildings, and of natural scenery.

The views which men cared about were not only within the town. One cannot but be aware that Edinburgh is part of its surroundings, and that its surroundings are part of Edinburgh. The stupendous rock of the Castle, Arthur's Seat, Calton Hill, the silver waters of the Firth of Forth in the distance — all these are part of the impact which the visitor to Edinburgh feels: 'la plus intéressante de toutes ces beautés . . . c'est la vue d'Edimbourg dans tout son ensemble, avec son couronnement admirable de montagnes.'[3] To some extent, the architecture of Edinburgh is not its greatest claim to fame. There is splendid architecture in Edinburgh, but the strong effect of a singular character rests more on the orderly planning of the town as a whole – the New Town, that is – and of the bringing together in that town of man and nature. Man is kept in touch with nature, the great book of nature, open for all to read, where, the eighteenth century felt, the laws of God had been recorded.

Thus it is significant that Craig's plan bears a quotation from Thomson's *Seasons*:

See long Canals [there was to be a canal where the railway line now runs]
See long Canals and deepened Rivers join
Each part with each, and with the circling Main
The whole enlivened Isle.

20

Or again, Starke, in his *Observations*, argues that the practice of Claude and Poussin, in constantly combining trees and architecture in their paintings, shows that there can be no beauty where either of these objects is wanting. Therefore the town planners also should combine them. This reference is suggestive, for there is in the paintings of Claude a Virgilian element, a feeling, as Sir Kenneth Clark puts it, 'of a Golden Age, of grazing flocks, unruffled waters and a calm, luminous sky, images of perfect harmony between man and nature'.[4] Is it going too far to suggest that the New Town is, as it were, a realization of an ideal landscape of this kind, combining the intellectual order of classical architecture and regular planning with a prospect of nature, fields and trees and hills, laid out for man's delight like a gentleman's park? Some such idea was surely in Craig's mind when he incorporated in his plan the views south of Princes Street, and north of Queen Street. There is the same sort of vision where the Queen Street gardens are retained, where the Calton Hill is kept as a walk and open space, where Lord Moray's pleasure grounds still slope, steeply wooded, to the banks of the Water of Leith: the vision of an earthly paradise, of the harmony between man and nature which the Enlightenment felt was both natural and desirable: man in touch with nature, and yet distinct.

In French town development there is the feeling that man has subdued nature, that nature is allowed to appear in the town but only in an orderly and subordinate form. But in Edinburgh there is this wonderful conjunction of grand natural views, trees, parks and buildings. Thus Edinburgh can be seen as a sort of evocation of an ideal, antique world, a city in which the attempt to reconstruct the Parthenon was the most natural thing imaginable. Men came to realize that what they had built was a modern Athens, an ideal city of the present which joined hands with

21

and was part of a golden age in the past.

These qualities of Edinburgh are hard to preserve, hard even for modern men to appreciate. The Enlightenment combined many things difficult to combine; nature and artifice; dignity and vitality; ambition and restraint. It was an age in many ways more civilized than our own. Where they had no shops we have many shops; where they had no businesses we have businesses; where they had no noise we have perpetual noise.

Yet much that is very fine remains in Edinburgh. If we neglect or destroy this great artistic expression of the Enlightenment, our successors will find it all the harder to escape from the pressures of our material age, and to re-capture the marvellous equilibrium, the sense of the dignity of nature and of human life which the men of the Enlightenment possessed and expressed.

[1] Carl L. Becker, *The Heavenly City of the 18th century Philosophers* (New Haven 1957), p. 34.

[2] T. Somerville, *My Own Life and Times, 1741-1814* (Edinburgh 1861), pp. 47-48.

[3] A. Blanqui, *Voyage d'un Jeune Français en Angleterre et en Ecosse* (Paris 1824), p. 249.

[4] Sir Kenneth Clark, *Landscape into Art* (London 1949), p. 65.

Hume, Reid, and
the Passion for Ideas

George Elder Davie

Let me begin with a pertinent question. This Scottish Enlightenment – was it an exotic bloom where Scotland was
concerned? How far was it the mere preserve of a leisure
class, which had immured itself in the New Town of
Edinburgh? This point of view, though still widespread, is,
I believe, seriously confused, being due to a failure to distinguish the aesthetic side of the Scottish Enlightenment,
as discussed by Professor Youngson, from the side I wish to
discuss: the passion for ideas. The artistic subtleties of the
townscape of the New Town – the Claude-Poussin effects,
for example, – may well have been exotics from a Scottish
point of view, but this remoteness from the nation was not
so true of the intellectual life. The ideas argued over at the
dinner tables of Charlotte Square, though they might derive
ultimately from the Universities of Germany or the Salons
of Paris, were eagerly overheard and assimilated throughout Scotland, and freely commented on and criticized by
persons of the most varied backgrounds.

This nation-wide concern with ideas was a remarkable
state of affairs, and one which was perhaps responsible for

the Scottish Enlightenment's intellectual seriousness. Elsewhere enamoured of abstractions and oversimplifications, the philosophy of *les lumières* was able to impinge on Calvinist Scotland only by dint of redrafting its whole intellectual programme in a realistic version which would do justice to the complexities of the human situation. Welcoming the Enlightenment demand for radical transformation of the conditions of social life, the Scots at this time flatly rejected the simplifying philosophy of reductive empiricism which was everywhere the accepted vehicle of forward-looking policy; in its place, they developed a historically-minded realism, which, durable and profound, avoided the characteristic limitations of the eighteenth-century outlook.

This markedly individual, not to say exceptional, character of the Enlightenment in Scotland – for long overlooked in the English-speaking world – has been duly noted on the Continent. Following up a line started by Charles de Rémusat's classic study of *la philosophie écossaise*, Paul Hazard has pointed out that the Scots had no sooner made their debut in the intellectual movement of the eighteenth century, than they decisively overthrew and outdated its basic principles, imposing a new direction. Already by 1730, Francis Hutcheson, father of the Scottish Enlightenment, was critical of Lockeian empiricism, which everywhere else in Europe was beginning to be the recognized standard. Taking up where Hutcheson left off, David Hume, in his *Treatise of Human Nature*, 1739, shattered beyond repair the whole basis of the principle of Enlightened rationality. Responding to his challenge, Thomas Reid and Adam Smith quickly carried through a radical reconstruction – in 1764 and 1775 respectively – which left the eighteenth century behind it: the first preparing the way for the *classe de Philosophie* era, and even for modern French Phenomenology, the second lucidly pointing forwards to the industrial society with its problem of 'alienation' and atomization.

Elsewhere the *siècle des lumières* was confidently brilliant; in Scotland, the modern world had already begun.

Taking for granted, as the distinguishing quality of the Scottish Enlightenment, this ability to look beyond eighteenth-century limits, I want to raise the question of the peculiarly national experience which at once stimulated Scottish far-sightedness and kept it looking in fruitful directions. In order to get light on this matter, it is, I believe, essential to bear in mind a circumstance which is too often forgotten – that the impact of the European Enlightenment on Scotland coincided precisely with the difficult post-Union decades, when Scotland was struggling to adapt, to the exigencies of the new political partnership with England, a native inheritance of institutions which had been conceived on Continental lines, partly through the Franco-Scottish connection, partly through contacts with the Netherlands. It was, one might say, this practical experience of adapting un-English institutions to the Union that made the Scots so very reserved in their recognition of the glowing promise of the Enlightenment. In this way, *la crise de conscience Européenne* (as Paul Hazard called it), the all-out intellectual revolt against the Baroque legacy of the seventeenth century, was limited and modified in its impact on Scotland by the counter-experience of a sort of *crisis of national existence*, in which the threat or reality of assimilation to England brought home, to the Scots, the value of their native inheritance of institutions, legal, ecclesiastical, educational.

In order to show how the Scottish Enlightenment fused national with intellectual aims, let us take Francis Hutcheson's neglected but important pamphlet of 1735 – *An Address to the Gentlemen of Scotland*. A sort of manifesto of the Scottish Enlightenment, this remarkable document takes as its starting-point the spiritual crisis, which, brought on by the Union, was in process of disrupting the established pattern of Scottish polity. The specific question at issue, as Hutcheson posed it in his pamphlet, was whether, under the London-centred incorporation of the two countries, the English arrangement of subordinating the Church to the State might not undermine the very different Scottish system which, modelled upon Continental example – not just Calvin's Geneva, but also the Dutch reform, as well as French protestantism in its legalized period – involved a delicately maintained balance between the democratic rights of the people and the authority of the state. The danger of Scottish assimilation to England in this spiritual sphere was, Hutcheson felt, not a merely theoretical one. A decree of the London Parliament, carried through in defiance of the Act of Union, had put effective control of Scottish ecclesiastical patronage in the hands of the crown, not only depriving Scottish congregations of their established right in the matter of appointing ministers, but in addition nullifying the influence of the Scottish gentry. More and more a situation had developed, Hutcheson thought, in which Scottish pulpits would be filled, not by well-educated Presbyterian pastors who would give a hand to the cause of the country's improvement, but by new Government placemen, whose overriding aim was simply to keep things quiet, thereby inducing the Church of Scotland to forget its progressive heritage as a leading part of the Calvinist-Presbyterian internationale, and to turn itself into pale imitations of the conformist and erastian Church of England.

The *never-to-be-forgotten Hutcheson*, as his admiring pupil, Adam Smith, was to call him, succeeded in establishing the credit of the Enlightenment among the sober-minded Scots, only because he was able, in declarations like the one under review, to present the illuminist principles in such a way that they seemed the sole viable answer to the post-Union spiritual crisis. Appealing to the national spirit of the Scots, dormant since the Union, Hutcheson outlined

26

a programme for the moral and material advancement of Scotland. Refusing to allow the anti-Union platform of the Jacobites a monopoly of Scottish nationalism, Hutcheson called for a liberal-minded patriotism which would operate within the framework of the Union. The lairds and smaller gentry, instead of, as heretofore, shirking their public responsibilities, must put themselves forward as the defenders and promoters of the cause of the nation. The first necessity, he emphasized, was to check the Anglicizing assimilation which, set in motion by the crown authorities, was sapping the spirit of the people. But at the same time, it was also necessary for the lairds to hold the nation together, in the face of the opposite danger of one of these retreats into sour-faced individualism, to which the Calvinist-minded democracy of Scotland was always excessively prone. If Scotland was to be a *progressive* nation, and not a backward one – and this Enlightenment principle was foremost in Hutcheson's mind – it was necessary that the spiritual leadership of the country should belong neither to Government-paid nominees intent on the *status quo*, nor to wild-eyed enthusiasts, eager to bring back the anarchy of Covenanting times.

How was this policy of patriotism within the Union going to attack the problem of Scottish backwardness? According to Hutcheson, the key to the situation lay in the proper employment of Scotland's native institutions – especially the Universities which, recently reorganized on the Netherlands model, constituted her chief national asset. The main thing to be watched here, Hutcheson argued, was that the democratic policy of the open door, valuable in itself, should not be allowed to conflict with the aim of improving the intellectual standards of the Universities. What the Universities must aim at was the production of ministers with sufficient culture and general education to enable them to co-operate with the lairds in promoting the cause of general

27

progress. In this way, Hutcheson's policy for a national-minded, liberal-minded Enlightenment provided a background to the ethics of public spiritedness which was to be the centre-piece of his Moral Philosophy.

The idea of a limited nationalism which Hutcheson put forward as the platform of a Scottish Enlightenment, was, however, at best, premature; and the compromises he called for began to break down in the tense years which led up to 1745. But this time completely out of patience with the Union, a considerable section of the Scottish nation was preparing to re-establish parliamentary independence by force of arms, restoring the Stuart dynasty and reviving the Franco-Scottish alliance. In this decade of plots and counter-manoeuvres, young Scotsmen of talent, instead of rallying to Francis Hutcheson's appeal for unity in the name of nationalism of the spirit, were preparing to take opposite sides in an imminent civil war; and the rising of '45 saw the economist-to-be, Sir James Steuart, busy at Holyroodhouse as Prince Charles' adviser, while the future philosophical historians, Adam Ferguson and William Robertson, rallied to the Government side in defence of the Union.

It was during this critical decade, when Scotland found herself faced with the unendurable alternatives of continuing the English Union (with all its humiliations) or of resuming the French alliance (with all its dangers) that the challenging genius of David Hume suddenly emerged, to generalize his country's experience of inextricable dilemma, into a profound critique of the basic Enlightenment principle of intellectual optimism. His studies at la Flêche, his business experience at Bristol, had already acquainted him, at first hand, with the divergence between the extroverted Baconian spirit of the English and the inward-looking Cartesianism found across the Channel. Inspired by this experience to anticipate, indeed to improve upon, the Kantian insight that this contrast between Continental

28

rationalism and English empiricism constituted a fundamental cleavage in the human point of view, David Hume
summed up the situation in that remarkable concluding
chapter to the *Treatise*, Book One, by opposing to one another, a pragmatic attitude recognized as typically English,
and an intellectualist attitude associated with France and
the Continent, as at once complementary to one another
and yet mutually irreconcilable. The essence of human intelligence, he says, consists in the precarious and perhaps
impossible balancing-act, of alternating between two rival,
incompatible positions – on the one hand a Cartesian intellect which will be satisfied with nothing but clear and
distinct ideas, and which seeks ultimate system; on the other
hand, an Anglo-Saxon pragmatism which has no time for
theory, and instinctively knows not to press the argument
too far. Confronting the apostles of the Enlightenment with
these irreconcilabilities and antinomies whose existence they
had so jauntily ignored, David Hume – here too forestalling
Immanuel Kant – bade them rethink their intellectual
foundations. Until they faced up to this ultimate contradiction between the intellectual factor and the pragmatic, their
optimism of civilization was based on the blindness of bad
faith.

Preoccupied with undermining the Enlightenment in its
global setting, Hume's philosophy was, nevertheless, especially destructive of the particular version which Hutcheson was trying to put over in Scotland. From Hume's point
of view, the pair of contrasting positions which Hutcheson,
intent on a media via, had condemned as extravagant ex-
tremes – on the one hand, the intellectual indifferentism of
pragmatic-minded Anglican conformists, and, on the other
hand, the soaring, insatiable quest for metaphysical clarity
à la Descartes, which Scottish Calvinists, following their
Continental brethren, regarded as the prerequisite of the
leap of faith – were, each in their different ways, far more

29

defensible and far more profound than the all-reconciling middle way which Hutchesonians recommended as the alternative to either. Confronted with clerical critic from the anti-Calvinist, Hutchesonian camp, Hume retorted by avowing his intellectual solidarity with the seventeenth-century French divines whom orthodox Scottish Calvinists admired – men like Huet, Bishop of Avranches, who approached religion by way of the metaphysical intellectualism of unsatisfied Cartesian self-doubt. Then, having thus administered this first shock to the Scottish Enlightenment by identifying with a position it regarded as a morbid scepticism, Hume went on to deal an even deadlier blow to its pride of intellect. Agreeing that the Continental ideal of the pursuit of absolute clarity, however well-founded, and as he believed, justifiable, nevertheless in the last analysis led to the most intolerable scepticism, he pointed out to the apostles of Enlightenment that the proper answer to the sceptical regress wasn't the apparatus of self-conscious intellectuality of which Scottish educationists were so fond, but the deliberately unintellectual attitude of the pragmatic Englishman. The Enlightenment had, Hume went on, gone astray in picking the would-be philosophical Francis Bacon as the Englishman most worthy of admiration. On the contrary, the sort of Englishman Europe should honour was the one it least appreciated – the unreflective country gentleman of the type of Addison's Sir Roger de Coverley, who had no interest whatsoever in philosophical first principles.

Passing from metaphysics to ethics and economics, Hume's genius, with a final characteristic flourish, completed the discomfiture of Enlightenment optimism, by a sort of Manichaean interpretation of human history, which sees it as a battle-ground between much the same pair of contrasting and sometimes complementary principles as we have already encountered in his metaphysics – the one down-to-earth and pragmatic, the other a counter-principle of an intellectual nature which aspires to a sort of metaphysical order and unity. The materialist conception of history, with its reductive, economic explanations, is, Hume allows, fruitful and satisfactory in regard to those institutions where the pragmatic principle is uppermost. However, there is, at the same time, always the limiting factor (too much overlooked by sociologists and economists) that the operation of the pragmatic principle of Enlightened self-interest tends to be cut across by the metaphysical counter-principle which, fastening on to and exploiting the religious side of experience, inspires various fanaticisms.

Applying this point of view to the social experience in which he was crucially caught up – the Scottish post-Union experience – Hume proceeded to formulate a view of the problem of Anglo-Scottish symbiosis which contradicts every principle put forward by Hutcheson. Putting himself first at the pragmatic point of view, Hume argues that there is no difficulty in principle as to how backward Scotland is to catch up with her richer neighbour. Given sufficient time and scope, *free trade*, by its automatic operation, would achieve the miracle. There is, therefore, no need of an organized national effort to reawaken the Scottish public-spiritedness, such as Hutcheson postulated. On the other hand, Hume is perfectly aware that this pragmatic point of view is only a partial one. Correcting it by bringing into view the metaphysical aspirations of man, we must bear in mind how the dark fanaticisms of the Scots could interfere with the beneficial automatisms of free trade. Difficulties of this kind might, no doubt, seem to warrant some state-interventionism, but, in any case, the appropriate kind of remedy here (if indeed any remedy is possible) would, Hume thinks, be found not so much in the kind of scheme Hutcheson favoured – encouragement, by the state, of liberal education – but, in the very arrangement Hutcheson most abhorred: a state-subsidized clergy, somewhat on the

31

Anglican plan. A comfortable, pragmatic parson, who knows on which side his bread is buttered would, Hume thinks, provide a far more promising check on Scottish fanaticism than a restlessly meddlesome clergy who pride themselves on their general education and liberal view.

Overlooked by the rest of Europe, the force of Hume's philosophy was first felt at home. An affront to everything the Scottish Enlightenment stood for, the Humian scepticism had aroused instant opposition among progressive-minded Scots of the Hutcheson type, who henceforth made it their chief intellectual aim to face up to this disconcerting blend of the most outrageous provocation and the most genuine profundity. To begin with, adequate answers to the *Treatise* were hard to come by, but, in the fifties, Lord Kames made a first break-through; and, with the advent of Adam Smith and Thomas Reid, the Scots not only managed to regain their shaken intellectual confidence, but were able to alert the Continental countries to the weaknesses in the Enlightenment system which had been uncovered through Hume's criticisms. In this sense, the European reaction against the excesses of eighteenth-century illuminism not only started in Scotland, but found in *la philosophie écossaise* some of its sanest and most influential exponents.

If we are to do justice to the long-continued Continental impact of the Scottish sequelae to Hume, if we are to appreciate why, even in the nineteenth century, a man of Théodore Jouffroy's stature could insist that *l'Ecole d'Edimbourg* had a central, not a merely exotic, interest to Europe, it is essential always to bear in mind that the historical background not merely to Hume's writings but to those of his chief Scottish critics – *le bon Thomas Reid* and the sequacious Dr Smith – was a Scotland which had been reinvolved in Europe as the result of the '45, and which had been reminded by the rising of the foregone and almost forgotten possibility of disconnecting itself from England, and renewing its Continental ties. From the European point of view, perhaps the most interesting and original feature of Scottish Philosophy was this – that the experience of revolt had made the Scots acutely aware of the profound intellectual cleavage, so shocking to Enlightenment optimism, between the values the English stood for, and those upheld by the Continentals. Found even in writers who were passionately concerned to reassert and realize the Union, like Adam Ferguson and Principal Robertson, this abstract Scottish critique of English insularity, this generalized view of the Union as, in some sense, a betrayal of Europe, gets its clearest expression from those writers who took the other side and endured exile in consequence. What Hegel and Marx, therefore, would find to interest them in the writings of the Scottish Jacobite leader, Sir James Steuart, whom they both admired so much, wasn't just a system of economics different from Adam Smith's, but an outspoken preference for the Continental principle of a conscious inwardness, preoccupied with the intellectual ideal of *system*, as against the contrasting English values of piecemeal, pragmatic procedures which are uninterested in anything but externals.

Adam Smith was, in his own way, as deeply involved as his fellow-economist, Sir James Steuart, in this critique of English insularity, and makes it the central theme of one of the most important and original sections of *The Wealth of Nations*. Taking up David Hume's economic question as to whether backward Scotland, under the free-trade conditions provided by the Union, could ever catch up with the immense superiority of her predominant partner, Adam Smith pointed that the question, posed in that form, attributes far too much advantage to England, and forgets certain counterassets which Scotland and other countries like Scotland could count upon. Drawing upon his experiences, as a student, of being educated, partly under the exclusive system peculiar to England, and partly under the more open system which the Scots had developed after Continental Calvinist models, Adam Smith was able to see clearly (what few at the time discerned) that a scheme of state-supervised, compulsory, elementary education on lines pioneered by Scotland, and other Presbyterian countries, was very well suited to the coming era of industrialization and the factory-system, not only as a means of *technical* training but even as a specific against 'alienation'. By reason of this educational differentiation, Scotland had, thus, a very definite economic asset which England lacked; and the Scots, if they cultivated properly this advantage, might hold their own in the otherwise difficult free-trade relation with England. Taking a remarkably penetrating and far-sighted view of social-intellectual factors, Adam Smith thus answers Hume's problem about free trade.

But what of Hume's lurking fear that fanaticism of spirit might interfere with the beneficent long-term effects of free trade? Conceding that there was a certain danger of this, Adam Smith went on to reject Hume's suggestion that a state subsidy to the clergy was the proper way to check public fanaticism. In the modern world, Smith argues, community-leadership wasn't a monopoly of the ministers of religion, but was the accepted responsibility of the professional classes generally. If the state was to disourage the narrowness of fanatical views, its aim should be not the out-of-date and, in any case, ineffective remedy of a subsidy to pastors and priests, but an official injunction (to be ratified by state supervision) that the professional classes get not blinkered and merely specialized training, such as is all they received in England, but also general courses in science and philosophy such as might encourage a balanced view of the human situation. Having begun by recommending, to the world public, elementary education more or less on the Scottish model, Adam Smith rounds off this system of a pedagogy for a modern, industrialized society by a generalization based on the social function of universities in Scotland.

This shift of emphasis from the clergy to the laity, and from religious and confessional instruction to general public education, was the capital contribution whereby Adam Smith, improving on his admired master, Francis Hutcheson, was able to turn the tables on Hume's sceptical pessimism, and point towards a scheme of Enlightenment more viable than that of the eighteenth century. What Adam Smith had done was reformulate Hutcheson's scheme of patriotism within the Union so as to give Scottish education pride of place over religion. But at the same time, in this doctrine of the relation of education and industry, Adam Smith, with his generalizing power, had more than Scotland in mind, and was giving the lead to a revolution which, carried through in nineteenth-century Europe, was to make Professors and school-masters, rather than priests and ministers, the responsible sources of public illumination.

Consequent on the insights of Adam Smith, the Scots, always education-minded, began to take very seriously the Continental affinities of their pedagogical system, confidently preferring it to the insularity of English arrangements. Whereas David Hume, with an eye to social advantages within the Union system, was in favour of sending Scottish boys of good family to English Eton, other representative Scots (of comparable standing) considered that the cultural advantages of education in the Scoto-Continental style was something of supreme importance. Thus, Hume's friend, the Baron Mure, disapproving of the narrowly classic bias of English education, imported a tutor from France, who would give the boys a general and philosophical grounding in the Continental style. For social reasons, indeed, the boys had to be sent to Oxford for a term or two, but the Baron counteracted its effects by putting them to

35

Paris for an equal period as well as by arranging that their studies, in the one and in the other place, were to be supervised by a Francophile Scottish philosopher, George Jardine, later to be celebrated as the colleague and friend of Thomas Reid, as well as the revered teacher of men like Francis Jeffrey of the *Edinburgh Review*, and Sir William Hamilton.

Having learned from his experience as pastor and as University Professor that, increasingly, religion was the divisive factor, education the factor of unity, Thomas Reid, too, is to be understood as a partisan of that sort of patriotism within the Union which regarded the school system and the Universities as Scotland's central institutions. In his account of the University of Glasgow, he emphasizes, in the Adam Smith manner, the difference between the general and liberal education dispensed in the North, and the more exclusive arrangements of the South. At the same time, Reid is far from being an echo of Adam Smith, and, in his characteristic contributions to the Aberdeen curricular reforms, he unmistakably identified himself with a position of extreme intellectualism – far more characteristic of the Continent than of Britain, and very unlike anything in Adam Smith – which insists that all departments of higher study must converge on, and be crowned by, a central metaphysic of first principles.

Shaken out of his intellectual optimism by the *Treatise of Human Nature*, Reid developed a double-sided attitude to Hume, regarding him as a philosophical critic of consummate genius, and, at the same time, a dangerously unsettling influence. The achievement of Hume was to have brought to light certain fundamental and deep-seated contradictions which the Enlightenment had unthinkingly taken over from the Renaissance and the Middle Ages. The danger inherent in his achievement was that the Humeian presentation of these contradictions as absolute, as rooted in the nature of things, played into the hands of the party

36

which regarded human nature as containing an original flaw. What Reid feared about Hume was that Calvinist or as one might say 'Pascalian' vein implicit in the scepticism.

A bold and yet supremely subtle intelligence, Reid directed his attention to the side of Hume from which Adam Smith had prudently held aloof – namely the metaphysical challenge. Was there indeed a sort of antinomy, an ultimate irreconcilability, between Continental intellectualism and English empiricism or pragmatism, as Hume had said, and as Kant, after him, was to agree? Avoiding the German solution of a higher synthesis which includes both, Reid sought a way out by means of a careful *distinctio* which, in these days of Husserl and phenomenology, has a very modern ring. Distinguishing sharply between science and philosophy, he pointed out that the intellectualist or Cartesian approach is true of the latter and false of the former, whereas the experimental or Baconian approach applies to the former, but not the latter. In a word, for Reid, it is the French who understand best about spirit, whereas the English are more at home in matter.

Elucidating the implications of this position for the philosophy of mind, Reid turned away from England and faced towards France. Taking a global view, he pointed out that not merely is there no serious contradiction between the English empiricist inheritance, and Continental Cartesianism, but, rightly regarded, the former is, in pure philosophy, only a sort of variant, an extreme aberration of the latter. Putting himself in a historical perspective, which sees the main stream of philosophical development as by-passing England, he next taught that the philosophical divergence which raised a really serious problem, was the conflict between the inheritance of Aristotle, and the pioneer effort of René Descartes to initiate a new start. Finally, with a cautious glance to the future, Reid looked forward to 'a

37

third age of man' which will advance beyond the second or Cartesian age, in much the same way as the latter was an advance on the first or Aristotelian. The slogan which inspired Reid's criticism of the Renaissance heritage as he prepared for the third age of man, was not, however, (as one might be tempted to think) 'Back to Aristotle', but 'Back to Descartes himself', and to the genuine original inspirations of Cartesianism. In the first place, Descartes was absolutely right in insisting that the philosophy of mind must have recourse to the inward-looking method of reflective analysis. The more external approach of the Aristotelians, Reid thinks, completely denatures mind by employing unscientific analogical methods which result in merely dispositional theories of human self-consciousness, such as compare the intelligence of man to the brittleness of a goblet. But in the second place, if we are to realize where Cartesianism went wrong, betraying its splendid start, it isn't enough to go to Descartes himself; we must also study the writings of his gifted disciples – especially the brilliant debate between Malebranche and Arnaud, which, Reid thinks, reveals, better than any other document, the real nature of the aberration of Europe's intellectual inheritance.

The stimulating sanity of this second version of the Scottish Enlightenment, due to the genius of Reid and Adam Smith, finally got through to Europe and America in the aftermath of the French Revolution. Welcomed by most countries, these Scottish ideas were nowhere more enthusiastically received than among the French nation, which, apart from the attraction of this novel platform of moderate and forward-looking liberalism, was duly impressed to find that its ancient Scottish allies, in spite of political separation, still remained spiritually faithful. The eighteenth-century Encyclopédistes had been, they now saw, premature in dismissing Scotland as once 'redoubtable' as a nation, but now, since the English Union, 'venal'. Perceiving that the venality was limited to political relations and, so far, did not touch essentials, men like Victor Cousin, Charles de Rémusat, Philarète Chasles made ample amends in their remarkable studies of culture in post-Union Scotland, thus setting in motion an intellectual current which has been splendidly maintained by Emile Boutroux in the 1900 epoch, and M. Maxime Chastaing in our own time.

Adam Ferguson and
the Idea of Community

Duncan Forbes

Adam Ferguson's *Essay on the History of Civil Society*, which was first published in 1767, is nowadays known to specialists only, though the author had a European reputation in his lifetime, and his books were translated into the leading European languages, not excluding Russian. For sociologists, the book is a classic; some regard Ferguson as the first proper sociologist; some think that his sociology is still relevant. Marxists, too, may remember him, because Marx quoted him with approval in *Das Kapital*. And it is this aspect of the *Essay*, not the more technical, sociological one, that I want to say something about; that is, Ferguson's critique of modern society.

The *Essay* is a study of the progress of society from rudeness to refinement, but at the same time the author is looking for a true criterion of civilization. It is concerned also with the problems of the 'declension' or decadence of nations; and with the relation between the progress of society and this.

Ferguson looks at the phenomena of social progress from different angles: there is the social scientist and psychologist observing and describing and making generalizations; there is the state-craft angle, in the tradition of the statecraft of Machiavelli, concerned with *virtù* or lack of it in a nation, the national vigour and capacity and defensive ability; there is the point of view of the moralist and humanist, concerned with what human nature truly is, and sensitive to signs of de-humanization and false values in modern society. All these points of view, though distinct, are interlocking.

In so far as it is concerned with the problem of decadence, Ferguson's book belongs to a type very common in the eighteenth century, in which, for instance, the contrast between modern luxury and selfishness and the virtues and public spirit of Sparta and republican Rome was constantly being drawn. Indeed this is one of the most deafening journalistic noises of the age. A shallow, commonplace idea, however, may fall sometimes into a deep pool of insight and suggestiveness – depending on the writer. And it happens that Ferguson was the only writer in the *genre* – the *Essay* was originally conceived, significantly enough, as a 'Treatise on Refinement' – who had inside knowledge and experience of a society, doomed certainly, and receding into the past, but still tight-knit, heroic, non-commercial.

He was a *Highlander*, son of the minister of Logierait, in Strathtay. The *Statistical Account* at the end of the century says that the parish is almost exclusively Gaelic-speaking. Ferguson spoke Gaelic, and was, for nine years, chaplain to the 42nd (the Black Watch). Thus the *Essay* is the work of an Edinburgh professor who was also a Highlander. There is nothing in the *Essay* itself to reveal this fact, no mention of the clan, but its Highland provenance throws into relief the fundamental question which, I suggest, was the real inspiration of the book: what happens to *man* in the progress of society? This question focuses all the various points of view just mentioned.

Ferguson's idea of human nature is interesting, unusual

41

in many respects for the eighteenth century. It consists, he says, of a number of characteristic propensities or 'drives', and it is not for the psychologist to single out any particular one as more fundamental than the rest. So that self-preservation or fear of death, for example, are powerful drives, but no more so than others such as ambition, love, loyalty to the group. And, anyway, in real experience feelings of pleasure and pain play a very minor role, because man is nothing if not an essentially active being, and when he is in action he is simply not conscious of feelings of pleasure or pain. And he is a creature who finds his happiness not in the attainment of his goal, but in the struggle towards it. He enjoys risk and danger, contention, hardship, and difficulty; his games and pastimes show this. He is progressive, because he is never satisfied; he always wants something better.

But the crucial thing for Ferguson is that men are fully human, reach their full potentiality as human beings, only when exerting themselves to the utmost – all their powers and capacities stretched to the full, wholly occupied – in and for the community of which they form a part, but in which they are not conscious of any apartness. Above all else, man is a community animal; and this is not to be explained away by a reference to mutual aid or self-interest. Men will often be found most attached to their community when the advantages of belonging are fewest, and the unnatural phenomenon of a detached, non-social being will be found, if anywhere, in the most civilized societies.

This sense of belonging to his group gives a man a kind of extra power and energy – it is not just a herd instinct – and it is called forth especially, and enhanced, when the group or society is threatened by danger, external or internal. This is why really great creative art and literature is the product of turmoil and crisis, not leisure, because at such times the sense of community is at its strongest.

Community, in fact, is Ferguson's criterion of real civilization. Look, he says, at the Greeks; in many respects, in their material conditions of living, in their conduct of war, they were grossly uncivilized.

But they lived, and died if necessary, for their little, incessantly feuding, communities, in perpetual danger and hardship, and this explains their achievements.

Now it is precisely community that is likely to be a casualty in the progress of civilization. What Ferguson has especially in mind is the danger of the desire and ability to combine for political purposes being weakened and destroyed by *indifference*. But the net is cast much wider than this, because community is the root of every aspect of civilization that really matters. It follows from what has been said so far, that if you destroy community, you destroy man's essential humanity and equilibrium and happiness.

The progress of society presents a three-pronged threat to community. There is the division of labour, without which the progress of society would be impossible; there is the social inequality which results; and there is the political tranquillity which is the result of commercial and industrial progress, and necessary to its further continuance.

In the *Essay*, Ferguson is, among other things, asking his contemporaries to take another look at their boasted achievements and values; their enlightenment, 'civility' and 'refinement'; the alleged political blessings of the 'matchless' constitution, on which the English so prided themselves; their possibly blind confidences and dangerous sense of security behind the shelter of the rule of law and free institutions. As he sees it, it is precisely the *achievement* of political liberty, free institutions, law and order, that is the real danger. He was a realist. He had studied Montesquieu. He knew that in the large, complex, economically advanced states of modern Europe, you could not normally expect the public spirit and whole-hearted devotion to the state, that in the republics of antiquity was only made possible by

43

primitive economic conditions. In the struggle of the seven-teenth century, Englishmen fought for liberty because they were fighting to protect their property and their profits. But liberty having been achieved, it is now possible for men to devote all their energies to profit-making, commercial activity, manufactures, in a word, to purely private concerns. As a result, they are in danger of losing the ability to com-bine for any purpose whatever. And laws and free institu-tions are in themselves no guarantee of liberty.

Ferguson also believed that whereas men's energies and interests can falter and fail on the artistic and literary sec-tors, on the technological, industrial, commercial sector the possibilities of progressive achievement are limitless, so that man's restless striving gets diverted more and more into that particular channel.

The result is a totally commercialized ethos. As Adam Smith said, in a passage in the *Wealth of Nations*, which has not, so far as I know, attracted much attention; *in a commercial society, every one is in some way or other a merchant*. And, Ferguson goes on, men's sense of values gets distorted. They come to value order, efficiency, moderation in politics, peace and quiet, above all else. They congratulate themselves on not having the misfortune to live in times of violence and civil war, forgetting that these things, though real evils, may be the result of passionate conviction, un-selfish loyalties, ability to combine, and may therefore be a sign of health and vigour in a nation.

Of the Greeks, for example, Ferguson writes in a peculi-arly Nietzche-like passage: 'If their animosities were great, their affections were proportionate; they, perhaps, loved, where we only pity; and were stern and inexorable, where we are not merciful, but only irresolute.'

Violent conflict, division in a nation, may be a sign of vigorous community life; peace and unity, of its total ab-sence. What looks like the good sense of the politically mature citizen may be the indifference of the hundred per cent bourgeois, wholly absorbed in his private concerns; and from him that hath not shall be taken away even that which he hath, if this indifference should result in the loss of his liberty.

This political indifference of modern commercial man is further encouraged by what we should call bureaucracy: the division of labour transferred from the commercial to the political sphere. For Ferguson, the paradox of making efficiency the supreme value was that the result was inefficiency. The routine mind was at a loss in any real emergency. He points out in this connection that the decadence he is talking about has nothing to do with effeminacy: dandified young men on the American frontier become as tough and resourceful as the Indians themselves. The implication seems to be that the 'youth is basically sound' argument is a red herring.

Ferguson's thinking on the evils of the division of labour is coloured by Machiavellian and classical notions: it is the separation of the soldier and the statesmen, the soldier and the citizen, that especially alarms him. One of the things that Ferguson was always passionate about was the lack of a Scottish militia – he started a club called the Poker, to stir up this issue. But what must be noticed in this connection is that it is not only patriotism, or liberty, or national defence, that is at stake. The humanist and moralist are involved, because Ferguson says that when the citizen surrenders his arms to the professional soldier, he surrenders an essential part of his humanity, and given Ferguson's account of human nature, one can see that this is so.

Man being what he is, when a citizen is exclusively a citizen and a mercenary soldier exclusively a mercenary soldier, both are something less than fully human. And again, the moral is that if efficiency is the only consideration, the result is something less than efficient. The pure professional will not be so good a soldier as the citizen-soldier fighting for everything he holds dear.

What is especially interesting about this for the historian of ideas is that he can discern here the first clear announcement of one of the most explosive themes in the history of modern thought; the idea of *alienation*, as it is called, meaning very roughly this : that in creating the complex structure of civilization, man has created something, without anyone willing it, in which he can no longer recognize his humanity, which is no longer a society in which he shares, but something which stands over against him, alien to him ; and if he is divorced from his community he is divided against himself, and no longer whole. In this theme, as it was expounded by Hegel and especially Marx, a crucial role is played by the division of labour.

Ferguson shows how the division of labour makes a breach in society between what we should call the managerial class and the rest, who become simply unthinking cogs in the machine. 'Manufactures prosper most where the mind is least consulted, and where the workshop may, without any great effort of imagination, be considered as an engine, the parts of which are men.' And the gulf is widened still further by another aspect of the general distortion of values. For with the progress of commerce and manufactures, articles of conspicuous consumption are produced which only the wealthy can afford : men come to be rated not by what they are, but by what they possess. 'We transfer the idea of perfection from the character to the equipage.' Poverty becomes the greatest disgrace of all : 'the minds of men become perplexed in the discernment of merit', and the rat race gathers momentum.

I have singled out only one aspect of Ferguson's thought, because it is not the sort of thing that people expect to find in the Scottish thinkers of the eighteenth century. Nor is it a peripheral matter; nor was Ferguson's a voice crying in the wilderness: indeed it appears to have been Adam Smith who first broached the potentially explosive topic of the effects of the division of labour.

I would just like to suggest that Ferguson spoke with some additional insight and authority, because it was easier for him than for his Lowland friends, to grasp the point that the good life is not necessarily impossible without economic progress, as his friend Hume thought, and that real civility, at any stage of social evolution, depends on community, even perhaps at the expense of unity.

Scott and
the Community of Intellect

The Hon. Lord Cameron

The half century that followed the last Rising for the Stuart cause saw the most brilliant flowering of the Scottish genius in Letters, Philosophy, Law, and in the practical arts of the architect and engineer. And yet all this sprang from a country divided in itself, where the ancient antipathy between Saxon and Gael, Highlander and Lowlander remained unhealed – and the embers of civil war still glowed red and resentful. Shorn of political coherence and unity by the Act of Union, Scotland had not found a common political voice or aim (indeed it may be doubted if she has yet done so): and domestic political controversy was directed to the aridities of ecclesiastical conflict. On the other hand the tide of material prosperity and of economic growth had already begun to flow : the merchants of Glasgow were looking hopefully towards the West; the energy and enterprise of a Justice Clerk – Fletcher of Milton – had stimulated the linen trade, the efforts of Roebuck and Cadell in the Chartered Carron Company gave new impetus to the industry of iron founding as well as adding a substantive to the vocabulary of war. The population was rising fast – in 1755 the population of Edinburgh totalled 57,000 whereas in 1792 it had risen to 85,000 while in the same period Glasgow's rose from 24,000 to 62,000.

Of the disparity between the Lowland and Highland Scot Dr Johnson wrote in 1773: 'To the southern inhabitants of Scotland the state of the mountains and islands is equally unknown with that of Borneo or Sumatra. They are strangers to the language and the manners and wants of the people whose life they would remodel and whose evils they would remedy.' Not all the evils which Dr Johnson noted in 1773 have even yet been remedied by 'the southern inhabitants'. Yet, at the same time, in face of their manifest diversity, in spite of the surrender of independent political sovereignty, there still remained the acceptance of the idea that Highland or Lowland, Saxon or Gael, were and remained *Scotsmen*, subjects of an ancient kingdom whose unity – precarious and hardly enforced though it may have been – still commanded a deep seated if not always unbroken loyalty. It was upon such a country with such continuing divisions but with such promise and presage of material improvement and prosperity that the impact of the Enlightenment fell and sparked off such a chain reaction of brilliance as Scotland never knew before – or indeed since.

This release of energy, mental as well as physical, would have been remarkable enough in any country, but when it is recalled that at the mid-century the total population of Scotland only just topped $1\frac{1}{4}$ million, the vigour as well as the consequences of this reaction to stimulus was and remains probably unique in the history of western civilization. The parallel of classical Greece, however, is perhaps obvious and possibly accurate, except that the flowering of the Greek genius, the real glory that was Greece, came in an age of political independence, though of marked and disastrous disunity. On the other hand the questing, schismatic, and sceptical qualities of the Greek mind have their parallel in certain notable Scottish characteristics, which go some way to explain why an intellectual movement which so markedly stimulated freedom of thought and promoted sceptical examination of institutions, principles and beliefs exercised such an influence of release in Scotland.

This galvanic surge of intellect made itself felt in almost every field of endeavour and thought. At the same time there are certain notable exceptions – especially the field of politics. The political sky was not star-studded with Scotsmen; no Burke nor even a Sheridan illumined thought or coruscated in debate. Mansfield, who might have scaled the political heights, preferred the serenity and safety of the Chief Justice's Chair to the precarious eminence of the Woolsack – with great profit to the development of the mercantile law of England. It is with political management and the exercise of patronage – to the great advantage of many young and ambitious Scots – that the name of Dundas is associated rather than with any profundity of political thought or with the higher achievements of statemanship. As law and politics, or at least its practice, have for so long been associated, this is strange, at first sight, since so much of the activity in Scottish life and letters sprang from this association with the practice of the law.

This interweaving of activity was not in any sense a unique phenomenon. Diversity of interest and achievement was marked in these generations, particularly in Scotland. It was of course much more easy then for a man of brilliance to be a polymath, a circumstance which made the essential unity of the whole world of learning – and indeed of civilized life – more easy to accept and recognize. It would not be easy today in the span of one academic career to combine in succession a University lectureship in Rhetoric and Belles Lettres, occupation of chairs of Logic and Moral Philosophy, and the preparation and publication of a world-famous treatise on economics – and to crown this academic career with the civil service appointment of Commissioner of Customs. This, however, was the career of Adam Smith: if unique in its particulars, it was characteristic of the width of competence of these men of the eighteenth century.

It may not be too extravagant to think that this very diversity of enterprise underlined the ultimate unity of intellectual effort and its roots in humanity's constant urge to probe deeper into the secrets of the natural world and its containing universe. And the Scottish system of education both in school and college may well have had a part to play in this, as well as the close knit texture of society in a country with so small a population that even in the last decade of the century the total population of the capital, then still its largest city, was just under 85,000. Enforced physical proximity in the Old Town of Edinburgh brought intimacy and recognition of a community of life; even philosophers were known by head-mark to the fishwives of Leith and Newhaven – you may recall the tale of the pious fishwife who refused aid to the atheistical David Hume in his miry predicament until he had repeated to her satisfaction the Lord's Prayer. One could scarcely expect a professorial humanist of these degenerate days either to obtain such instant recognition or to be required to purchase rescue from a similar predicament at such a price.

In such a society, close knit physically, socially and intellectually, when the lawyer could be a man of letters or historian or philosopher, the divine a dramatist, the wigmaker a poet and the philosopher a diplomat, the essential unity of the world of thought and action could readily be recognized and accepted with all its consequences.

The law of Scotland perhaps never produced many men of such marked diversity – not to say eccentricity – of character as in this brilliant age, and never did its develop-

51

ment receive such comprehensive and profound promotion. The men of law still live in anecdote and story – not surprising perhaps when one learned judge combined town planning with acute interest in agriculture, so acute indeed that he shared his bedroom with a pig, while another, famed for his learning, held firmly to the theory that all mankind were born with tails, but deprived of this appendage by midwives at birth. This eccentricity of conduct, however, was not confined to the profession of the law alone – was it not an eminent Edinburgh surgeon of the day who went his professional rounds accompanied by a pet lamb? On the other hand, there were judges who had like Lord Hailes earned solid reputations in the world of letters as historians, and the fame of Henry Home, Lord Kames, rested on a more solid philosophical basis than was due to his eccentricity of speech and manner. And it is not to be forgotten that the extraordinary Boswell was himself a practising advocate. Law and letters tended to go hand in hand: perhaps something was due to the length of vacation they enjoyed in the old Scottish Courts, which permitted leisure for the pursuit of literature as well as the improvement of agriculture by the many landowners who followed also the calling of the law. When in 1836 the old vacations of two months in spring and four in summer and autumn disappeared before the advance of reform, Cockburn made this note in his journal: 'It is this abdication from legal business which has given Scotland the greatest part of her literature that has adorned her. The lawyers have been the most intellectual class in the country. The Society of the Outer House has given them every possible incitement, and the Advocates' Library has furnished them with the means and the temptation to read. What a proportion of our eminent men have been trained in this scene!'

It was not however in the wider field of letters or philosophy that Scots lawyers made their greatest impact on the life of Scotland: the latter part of the eighteenth century saw a great moulding of the Common law of Scotland at the hands of writers whose work was immediately recognized as of classical importance and quality. Scotland was already fortunate that her Common law had been given philosophical cohesion and rational formulation in the institutional work of the great Lord Stair. The publication of his *Institutions* in 1681 laid the foundation of a system flexible and harmonious and readily capable of development and adaptation to the needs of a developing and changing society. Stair, philosopher, statesman and jurist, in his dedication of the work to King Charles II put his own view of the law of Scotland in terms I cannot refrain from quoting: 'For we are happy in having so few and so clear Statutes: our law is most part consuetudinary . . . and we always prefer the sense to the subtlety of law and do seldom trip by niceties and formalities.' And it was the third edition of Stair's *Institutions* published in 1759 which was the basis of young Walter Scott's legal studies – the course of which the reader may trace in the studious activities of Alan Fairford (who was of course Scott himself) in *Redgauntlet*.

It was on this foundation that the great works of later writers in the civil law of this country were erected – Erskine and later Bell: their institutional writings are still the classic sources of our Common law, supplemented in the field of crime by the Commentaries of Baron Hume. These three men are all men of that half century, Erskine's *Principles* being written in 1754 and his *Institute* published in 1773. Lawyers of succeeding generations – and indeed Scotland – owe a debt of perennial gratitude to these moulders and expounders of our native jurisprudence. It might have been happier and more fortunate had the flexible instrument thus created been permitted freely to adapt itself throughout the nineteenth century; free from the harmonizing interpolations from another system of law so essentially different in origin and development from our own. But this is another story.

It is on the rational basis from which the common law springs and which therefore demands acceptance as the cement of the fabric of society, that all these institutional writers lay their initial and continuing emphasis – as well as on its conformity with natural law or the law of nature. This was the Age of Reason no doubt, and it may well be that the impulse to find and express the rational essence of the law was not only consonant with but was derived directly from the spirit of the age. Yet this development of the law came in the same century and indeed but a few decades from the time when a judge of the supreme court – Lord Grange, brother of 'Bobbing John,' the Earl of Mar of the '15 – could arrange with a convenient friend – Lovat – for the sequestration of an unsatisfactory wife to the far island of St Kilda.

The marriage of law and letters, fruitful though it was in many directions, had its most remarkable issue in the genius of Scott. Scott the Romantic was a true child of this Age of Reason and it may be that his early acquaintance with German literature and poetry first turned his mind towards the work on which his fame came to rest and which gave him his literary influence. Indeed in his own words: 'The success of a few ballads had the effect of converting a painstaking lawyer of some years' standing into a follower of literature.' One reason why he concealed for so long his identity as the 'Author of Waverley' was, he said, 'I am not quite sure that it would be considered decorous in me as a Clerk of Court to write novels. Judges being monks, clerks are a sort of lay brethren from whom some solemnity of walk and conduct may be deemed proper.'

It is Scott the novelist, Scott whose work and influence upon the Romantic age gave him world-wide fame, who is most usually acclaimed. There is also Scott the poet, the historian and the man of affairs, but at the root of this diversity of talent and of genius was the *man of law*, and of Scots law at that. And Walter Scott himself was in a sense so typical a product of legal Edinburgh. His father a respectable W.S., in good practice, a man of presbyterian principle, his mother of a respected Scots family, he himself educated at Edinburgh's own High School and College, a practising advocate at the Scots Bar and a conscientious and experienced sheriff – whose origin, upbringing and calling could be more redolent of the life of the law or less likely to throw up a novelist of genius? Scott was not like Stevenson, whose practice at the Scots Bar consisted of one petition and whose knowledge of the civil law of Rome just enabled him to know that stillicide was not a crime nor was emphyteusis a disease: he was a practising lawyer familiar with the world in which life and law made contact in so many differing ways and with so many often curious consequences, and where human nature with its infinity of variation can display all its best as well as its worst qualities.

The world of Scott was a world in which men of genius and talent rubbed shoulders and indeed lived in a community of intellect where the language of specialization had not yet begun to erect those barriers which today in increasing degree inhibit the ease of effective communication in the world of thought and of the mind. One illustration taken from one of his own novels will serve. When in *Guy Mannering* Colonel Mannering first visits Edinburgh and calls on Counsellor Pleydell he received from him notes of introduction to some of Pleydell's Edinburgh circle, and 'Mannering was gratified to see that they were addressed to some of the first literary characters of Scotland, "to David Hume Esq.", "to John Home Esq.", to Dr Ferguson", "to Dr Black", "to Lord Kames", "to Mr Hutton", "to John Clerk Esq., of Eldin", "to Adam Smith Esq.", "to Dr Robinson" – a remarkable circle of friends for a busy member of the bar.' But this did not represent a fictional circle: this was the circle in which Scott and men like him habitually moved – historians, economists, dramatists, philosophers, lawyers – and among them men whose work was not only to illumine the age of Enlightenment but to have influence on the course of western civilization itself.

The life of Scott no doubt revolved about the law – but it was not a dry as dust compilation of ancient precedents or a proliferating forest of ill co-ordinated statutes: it was the historic law of a proud and ancient kingdom which had been in large measure fused into a coherent flexible and compendious scheme of jurisprudence by the earlier work of Stair and the later labours of John Erskine, a child of the Enlightenment. It is true that in 1785 at the tender age of fourteen Walter Scott in his own somewhat rueful words 'entered upon the dry and barren wilderness of forms and conveyances' – though these dry and barren forms – from Dallas of St Martins' Styles – came alive in *Waverley* in the hands of Bailie Duncan Macwheeble, the Baron of Bradwardine's 'doer'. The wilderness was not all dry and barren – it blossomed like the rose in those novels into which Scott put so much of his own knowledge of the law, its practice and its language. When he came to study Stair's *Institutions of the Law of Scotland*, I cannot but think that his imagination must have been fired and his pride of country roused by the majestic prose of that great master of the law.

'This nation', wrote Stair, 'hath not been obscure and unknown to the world; but the most famous nations have made use of our arms and have still in grateful remembrance retained trophies of our courage and constancy. There be few wars in Christendom wherein we have not had considerable bodies of soldiers regimented and commanded by themselves and oftimes general officers commanding them and whole armies of strangers, with great reputation and gallantry which did advance them above the natives of those countries whom they served.' Is not here the common ancestry of Quentin Durward and his Comrades of Louis XI's Scottish Guards, of Dugald Dalgetty, 'ritt-master' under that invincible monarch, the bulwark of the Protestant Faith, the Lion of the North, the terror of Austria, Gustavus the Victorious, and of the Baron of Bradwardine himself with his oft recounted service under Arabella Churchill's illustrious son the Marshal Duke of Berwick?

And would not his youthful patriotism have warmed to the flame that burns so strongly in all his writings by these words: 'We do not pretend to be among the great and rich kingdoms of the earth yet we know not who can claim preference in antiquity and integrity, being of one blood and lineage without mixture of any people and have so continued above 2,000 years – during all which no foreign power was ever able to settle the dominion of a strange lord over us.'

Indeed so much of Scott is Scots Law – its language, its form and its substance – the law called to the service of romance. Right from the first, *Waverley* is set within the boundaries of Scots feudal tenures and the operation of the Scottish feudal system itself – the tenure on which the Barony of Bradwardine was held and the detailed operation of the law of entail of land. *Guy Mannering*, vouched for on the authority of Saintsbury as 'best of the novels for merit of construction and interest of detail', was modelled from at least two current *causes célèbres* of the day concerning missing heirs – and again the operation of the law of entail. To cite one last further illustration, the *Heart of Midlothian* is contained within a legal framework – the criminal record of the Porteous Riots, and the law of concealment of pregnancy and child murder.

Law of course represents one side only of the life of Scotland. Yet in the jurists of this age of Reason law is related to the life and purpose of society: there was a certain unity in the spirit of the age; with all its scepticism and questioning of accepted beliefs and institutions. That questioning was at least fundamentally based upon a conception of the unity of society – with the silent implication of acceptance of a community of purpose. And for many at least there was a recognized binding force : citizens of the world of thought and learning they may all have been where no frontier challenged and the only passport was knowledge and an inquiring mind, but at the same time they were citizens of a Scotland which commanded their common allegiance. But the spirit of the age worked not only on the men of thought, of science, of letters and of the law, but in civic life as well. Edinburgh's life and future were radically influenced by her greatest Provost, Drummond, while the most distinguished bookseller of the century, himself a man of letters, of philosophic and speculative mind, William Creech, served his city well as Provost for more than one term. It was Drummond who had the vision of the New Town, a vision which he was able to realize, and who laid the foundations on which the great Infirmary of Edinburgh was able to build its fame and reputation.

The world owes many debts to the Scotsmen of the Enlightenment. These men left Scotland in particular three great legacies, the classic exposition of the law of Scotland, the fruits of the genius of Walter Scott, and the magnificence of the New Town of Edinburgh – legacies of which today we are still the beneficiaries, and in some degree the trustees.

Sydney Smith and
the Spirit of Criticism

Allan Frazer

In the mid-summer of 1798 the Reverend Sydney Smith, perhaps the most remarkable clergyman of the Church of England ever to visit Scotland, arrived in Edinburgh and took lodgings at 38 Hanover Street. Later he was to be described by Lord Jeffrey as the gayest man and the greatest wit in England; by Thomas Moore as a fellow of infinite fun; and by Macaulay not only as one of the most original writers of his time but as indeed the 'Smith of Smiths'.

All this, however, lay some way ahead. In 1798 at the age of twenty-seven he had been for three years the impecunious curate of Netheravon, a desolate Parish on Salisbury Plain, which he himself described as 'of a profound, unmeasurable and awful dullness'.

But if his surroundings were bleak and the poverty of his flock depressing there was nothing dreary about the curate himself. His geniality, good humour and independence of mind were quite out of the ordinary and it is hardly surprising that in such a melancholy setting they commended him to Mr Hicks Beech, the local Squire, with whose family he was soon on affectionate terms. Hicks Beech had a young son, Michael, with a couple of years to put in before going up to Oxford. Michael was a quiet and introspective youth who kept his own counsel and went to bed early, qualities which in one so young both the curate and his patron considered untimely. What could be more enlivening for the young man, thought his father, than a visit to the Continent with Sydney as guide and companion. The suggestion had only to be made for the curate to jump at it, and since Michael offered no resistance, arrangements were put in train to set out for the University of Weimar.

By one of the accidents of history, which was to have unpredictable consequences for Scotland and indeed far beyond, the plan was thwarted by the military operations of Napoleon which rendered the excursion inexpedient. But there was an obvious alternative. If they were to be denied the stimulus of Goethe and Schiller there was Edinburgh, where the rebellion against old ideas and the fermentation of new ones offered even more exciting prospects.

There are three invariable characteristics of periods of renaissance, which strikingly disclose themselves in the Edinburgh of this period. The first is that the excitement of new ideas transcends the conventional opposition between succeeding generations: the second that intellectual ferment is a social rather than an individual phenomenon. Genius may come to birth in isolation, but it can only grow to its full stature in a reciprocal society. And it enlarges itself as much by what it gives to sympathetic spirits as by what it receives from them. Finally, a renaissance is never merely an effervescence of the corporate intellect. To sustain itself it must issue in action: the abstract must become concrete and the general, particular. Let us see how these principles show themselves in the interaction between Sydney Smith and the society in which he found himself in Edinburgh about the year 1800.

He himself was of course stimulated by the restless intellectual vigour of the circle in which he moved, drawn mainly from the University and the Bar. Naturally he attended the lectures of Dugald Stewart and that 'curious and excellent man' Dr Gregory. But perhaps more surprising, Stewart in turn went to hear his student preach and afterwards had this to say about Sydney's sermon.

> His original and unexpected ideas gave me a thrilling
> sensation of sublimity never before awakened by any
> other oratory.

By any standards this must be considered most unusual compliment by a Professor to one of his students or for that matter by a man in late middle age to one still in his twenties. But given the right setting and provided the current is powerful enough, a spark can leap across a surprisingly large gap.

The interplay of diverse minds upon each other was fostered by numerous Clubs, of which one of the most famous was the *Friday Club* founded by Scott as a sodality of kindred spirits interested in literature and free from conversational aggressiveness, political bigotry, and religious narrow-mindedness. It contained most of the intellectually eminent men of the time, regardless of creed or party. Three of them – Sydney Smith, Francis Jeffrey and Henry Brougham – were to revolutionize the entire social pattern by the creation of the *Edinburgh Review*. Let Sydney, whose enthusiasm and vigour overcame the misgivings of Brougham and the timidity of Jeffrey, tell in his own words of its origin and results.

> Towards the end of my residence in Edinburgh
> Brougham, Jeffrey and myself happened to meet in the
> eighth or ninth storey at Buccleuch Place, the then
> elevated residence of Mr Jeffrey. I proposed that we
> should set up a review. This was acceded to with
> acclamation and I was appointed editor.

To appreciate its value the state of England at the period should be held in remembrance. The Catholics were not emancipated, the Game Laws were horribly oppressive, steel traps and spring guns were set all over the country, prisoners tried for their lives could have no Counsel, and the enormous wickedness of the slave trade was tolerated. . . . It was an awful period for those who ventured to maintain liberal opinions and were too honest to sell them for the ermine of the Judge or the lawn of the prelate.

A long and hopeless career in your profession, the chuckling grin of noodles, the sarcastic leer of the genuine political rogue, these were the penalties exacted for liberality of opinion at that period.

Not a murmur against any abuse was permitted. To say a word against the cruel punishment of the Game Laws or against any abuse which a rich man inflicted and a poor man suffered was bitterly and steadily resented.

If this oppressive catalogue now seems a little unreal it is largely because the *Edinburgh Review* created a climate of opinion in which the viciousness of national as well as personal tyranny became intolerable and was, as a result, put down. The importance of this fact for an understanding of the culture of Edinburgh in the Age of Reason — as David Craig has pointed out[1] — is that the *Edinburgh* (and indeed the *Quarterly*, in its Scottish origins) was in essence a means of communicating to a wider public the table talk of the Edinburgh salons at the turn of the century. The topics of the *Edinburgh* are those that engaged the civility at their dinner tables, or later in the less respectable milieux favoured by Christopher North; the range of interest is *their* range; the tone *their* tone. Just as television today offers us, say, the riches (such as they are) of a Royal Academy banquet, so the *Edinburgh Review* was in essence an extension and projection of the cultivated society from which it sprang. The important word to note is 'cultivated'. The ease of manner and expression that came to Sydney Smith as a birthright was still painfully alien to his Scotch associates. Nonetheless by the time the *Review* was founded, the Edinburgh Establishment had come to realize that peaceful penetration of England involved an acceptance of at least the more superficial of English *mores*. Among these was English speech, in distinction to the Edinburgh dialect of Scots that was still general. This English style was cultivated by Jeffrey and his circle in the *written* expression of their views; whereas, around the dinner table, they found freedom in their homelier native tongue. This effort towards a polite English allowed them to go so far but no farther in belles lettres; it could be handled by them in such a way as to make possible a vigorous and articulate criticism, but it was inept for the finest *creative* work. English was the language of the head; only in the vernacular were Burns and Scott free to let the heart speak. Thus the *Edinburgh* is at one and the same time an emblem of the achievement and limitation of the culture of the city of Edinburgh in the Age of Reason: and a very remarkable one, with a circulation of 13,000 copies per issue and a readership many times greater.

This made it a trenchant weapon of reform. What is the savour and particular quality of Sydney Smith's contributions to it? Certainly he speaks of himself as having a passionate love of common justice and common sense but these he shared with many of his radical contemporaries. How did he make them effective?

Perhaps a clue may be found in a letter which he wrote to Hicks Beech about Michael very early on during their stay in Edinburgh. The same technique which worked with him was equally successful in a far wider field.

My first serious conversation with him, wrote Sydney,

63

was upon the subject of his toilette and the very great portion of time he daily consumed in adorning himself. This Michael took in high anger and was extremely sulky; and upon my renewing the conversation some time after he was still more so. Without the smallest appearance of anger or vexation on my part I turned his Sulkiness into ridicule and completely laughed him into good humour.

This throughout his life was his method. He did not rail or scold but overcame his opponents either by reducing their propositions to absurdity or exposing the meanness of their views and practices to ridicule. Hesketh Pearson in his affectionate and perceptive study *The Smith of Smiths* has rescued numerous examples from the *Edinburgh Review* and elsewhere. Three may suffice, directed to objects as various as the Game Laws, the employment of young children as chimney sweeps, and one aspect of what many were at that time pleased to call English Justice.

Spring guns and mantraps were universally recognized among the landed classes as a perfectly proper mode of deterring the lower orders from any encroachment upon the preserves of their betters. Such appliances had received judicial approval and that indeed upon the weightiest considerations. A certain Mr Justice Best in the case if Ilot versus Wilks had solemnly expressed the view that the preservation of Game while desirable in itself had a further and even more important purpose:

This case has been discussed at the Bar, he observed, 'as if these engines were exclusively resorted to for the protection of Game; but I consider them as lawfully applicable to the protection of every species of property against unlawful trespassers. . . . I for one should be extremely glad to adopt such means, if they were found sufficient for that purpose; because I think it a great object that gentlemen should have a temptation

to reside in the country amongst their neighbours and
tenantry whose interests must be materially advanced
by such a circumstance. The links of society are thereby
better preserved, and the mutual advantage and
dependence of the higher and lower classes of society
existing between each other, more beneficially maintained. . . . By preserving Game, gentlemen are
tempted to reside in the country; and considering
that the diversion of the field is the only one of which
they can partake on their estates, I am of opinion
that for the purpose I have stated it is of essential
importance that this species of property should be
invoilably protected.'

Such pompous inhumanity from the Bench Sydney
Smith was not prepared to tolerate. This was his comment.

We do not suppose all preservers of game to be so
bloodily inclined that they would prefer the death of
a poacher to his staying away. Their object is to
preserve game; they have no objection to preserve
the lives of their fellow-creatures also, if both can
exist at the same time; if not, the least worthy of
God's creatures must fall – the rustic without a soul, –
not the Christian partridge – not the immortal
pheasant – not the rational woodcock, or the account-
able hare.

He loathed tyranny in any form, but more particularly
when directed to the weak and defenceless. The exploita-
tion of children as chimney sweeps roused his anger but
did not disturb his judgment. He perceived that the fault
was one not of brutality but of sheer thoughtlessness and
lack of imagination. This is how he brings the point home.

An excellent and well-arranged dinner is the most
pleasing occurrence, and a great triumph of civilized
life. It is not only the descending morsel, and the
enveloping sauce – but the rank, wealth, wit, and

65

beauty which surround the meats . . . The hour of dinner, in short, includes every thing of sensual and intellectual gratification which a great nation glories in producing. . . .

We come now to burning little chimney sweepers. A large party are invited to dinner – a great display is to be made; – and about an hour before dinner, there is an alarm that the kitchen chimney is on fire! It is impossible to put off the distinguished personnages who are expected. It gets very late for the soup and fish, the cook is frantic – all eyes are turned upon the sable consolation of the master chimney sweeper – and up into the midst of the burning chimney is sent one of the miserable little infants of the brush! There is a positive prohibition of this practice, and an enactment of penalties in one of the acts of Parliament, which respect chimney sweepers. But what matter acts of Parliament, when the pleasures of genteel people are concerned? Or what is a toasted child compared to the agonies of the mistress of the house with a deranged dinner?

And finally a glance at the English Courts. Prisoners accused of felony were not allowed to employ Counsel and this was justified on the argument that the prisoner would otherwise be involved in costs which he could ill-afford. Sydney's comment was in the form of a speech suitable to be delivered to a condemned man.

You are going to be hanged tomorrow, it is true, but consider what a sum you have saved. Mr Scarlett or Mr Brougham might certainly have presented arguments to the Jury which would have insured your acquittal, but do you forget that gentlemen of their eminence must be recompensed by large fees and and that if your life had been saved you would actually have been out of pocket about £20. You will now die

with the consciousness of having obeyed the dictates
of a wise economy and with a grateful reverence for
the laws of your country which prevent you from
running into such unbounded expense – so now let us
go to prayers.

Among lawyers, Scarlett and Brougham are still names
to conjure with. Their victories are buried in the Law
Reports. But Sydney Smith pleading with compassion and
wit at the bar of public opinion won verdicts for humanity
which are enshrined in the freedom of the common man.

[1] in, *Scottish Literature and the Scottish People.*

E Prelo Academico.

Edinburgh
and its University Press

The first book associated with the University of Edinburgh was published in 1596. The office of *Academiae Typographus* was established in the first half of the 17th century, and in 1637 the University granted George Anderson permission to set up a printing press in the College buildings. Thirty years later that press became more firmly established under the direction of George's son, Andrew; and, later, of Andrew's widow. Andrew obtained by royal patent the monopoly of bible printing in Scotland, and Mrs Anderson maintained her monopoly for many years, in the face of constant litigation. Albeit a wretched printer, she was a patriot, and we are indebted to her 'university press' for the record of the *Debates* that led up to the Act of Union (1707).

In the 18th century the great Edinburgh-based scholar printers – Ruddiman, Hamilton, Smellie, Creech – were all, in turn, 'printers to the University', Shortly after 1800 the colophon 'Edinburgh: at the University Press' came into general use, and appears in that form on the title page of Jamieson's great *Dictionary of the Scottish Language* (1808).

The present successor to these presses was established by the University Court in 1946, and is a learned press wholly owned and controlled by the University of Edinburgh. It has a current output of about 30 books per year, and an enviable reputation for important scholarship, careful editing, exacting production standards, and imaginative book design.

In the context of this pamphlet on the Enlightenment in Scotland it is appropriate to list the following recent publications:

THE DEMOCRATIC INTELLECT
George Elder Davie
Reader in Logic and Metaphysics, Edinburgh
This passionate and learned exposition of the principles of Scottish University Education, as they pertained at the close of the 18th century, and were slowly abandoned in the 19th as a result of social, political and economic pressures, has not merely attained classic status since publication in 1960, but has considerably influenced the educational philosophy of newly established universities both north and south of the Border. 50s.

ESSAY ON THE HISTORY OF CIVIL SOCIETY
Adam Ferguson
Edited by Duncan Forbes, Clare College, Cambridge
This handsome volume reprints the first edition (1767) of Ferguson's seminal *Essay*, with a collation of variants in the last edition (1814) to appear in the author's lifetime. In a scholarly introduction Duncan Forbes has scope to elaborate many of the aspects of Ferguson's thought which he touches upon in his paper in this pamphlet.   42s.

THE MAKING OF CLASSICAL EDINBURGH
A. J. Youngson
Professor of Political Economy, Edinburgh
Professor Youngson sets out to explain how a small, crowded, almost medieval town, the capital of a comparatively poor country, expanded in a short space of time, without foreign advice or assistance, so as to become one of the enduringly beautiful cities of Western Europe. This story of a vision made real is one of the most important, original, and fascinating contributions of recent years to urban studies. The text is lavishly provided with 18th and 19th century engravings, maps, plans and architects' drawings; and with a splendid set of photographs specially taken for the book by Mr Edwin Smith.   63s.

LETTER FROM A GENTLEMAN TO HIS FRIEND IN EDINBURGH
David Hume
Edited by E. C. Mossner and J. V. Price
It is appropriate in the context of this pamphlet to announce a slender but significant addition to the Hume corpus. In 1745 Hume applied unsuccessfully for the Edinburgh Moral Philosophy Chair (then called *Pneumatics*). His opponents used the alleged atheism of the *Treatise* against him. Hume wrote the *Letter* to defend himself against these attacks, and it was published as a 34 page booklet, in 1745. No copy had ever come to light till the National Library of Scotland acquired, in December 1966, the one of which this volume is a facsimile reprint. Professor Mossner has contributed a valuable introduction. The work will be published in autumn 1967.

69

Printed in Great Britain by
Robert Cunningham & Sons Limited, Alva